Reflections on Love and Wisdom

Short Essays from a Physician's Journey

Mark Bulgarelli

Copyright 2024

All Rights Reserved

Case Id:
14466495811

Table of Contents

Dedication

This book is dedicated to Simon and Andrew, and to James and John.

They were fishermen casting their nets when the Son of Man came along and said "Follow Me."

They became the first Fishers of Men.

I hope that this little book helps cast a bigger net.

About the Author

Mark Bulgarelli is a retired Internal Medicine physician. He practiced in Primary Care for over 30 years. His first 15 years of practice was among the indigent, uninsured, and marginalized populations in our country.

He is a former athlete having played baseball at the University of Arkansas and was a co-captain on the 1979 College World Series Team that finished as national runner-up. He spent 8 days in Lviv, Ukraine early in the Russia/Ukraine war on a medical relief team. In retirement, he is volunteering at his church mentoring young men, and also volunteering at a local hospital. He is on faculty at the California College of Science and Medicine teaching medical students and residents. He has 3 children and 2 dogs and lives in Menifee, California

Acknowledgements

The author would like to acknowledge those who were helpful getting these short essays together.

He has breakfast with several men weekly who reviewed many of these writings. In particular, he would like to acknowledge Oliver, Jim, Rich, both Mikes, Bob, and Janette V. for their support and input.

There were many others who saw these and made comments along the way. Please forgive me for not mentioning everyone's name.

And to Jessica, my oldest daughter, for her love and encouragement with this project.

And, as always, Carol.

Background of Lessons of the Day

This is for all of my friends who have started getting my little lessons of the day. Part of me feels like I owe you an explanation.

I started these lessons of the day many years ago when my children were young. It was an attempt for Daddy to influence their lives with love, goodness, and other good things. Most of those lessons revolve around a small Bible verse that I have found inspirational.

I put many of those things out to the kids during that time but then as they grew older I stopped doing it.

I've always had a little bit of an itch to write something, but I don't have a lot of discipline and skill in that realm.

A few weeks ago, as you know, I started doing it again and decided that this time I would not only include my children, but other people that were closest to me. I've known many of you for a long time and I can say that all of you have touched my life with love and goodness in one form or another. So I have come to this point in my life because of God and goodness, and also because of all of you and the love, patience, goodness, and understanding that you've shown me.

So that's what all of this is about.

I can't say that some of it's not therapeutic on my part as I reflect on God and His goodness and love in those verses, and then how I approach love and goodness in my own life.

I hope that you all find goodness, love, and may be a little inspiration in these short essays. I hope that they brighten your day just a little bit.

Thank you all for touching my life.

A Baby's Eyes

Good Morning, Brothers and Sisters.

"You are all children of the light and children of the day. We do not belong to the night or to the darkness." 1 Thessalonians 5:5

"Taking the child in his arms, He said to them, "Whoever welcomes one of these little children in my name welcomes me, and whoever welcomes me welcomes the Father who sent me." Mark 9:37

"Truly I tell you, anyone who will not receive the kingdom of God like a little child will never enter it." Luke 18:17

"Beware that you never look down on any of these little ones. I tell you that their angels are always in the presence of my Father." Matthew 19:10

A Baby's eyes.

We see it all there…

All the things that we need for the kingdom.

We are their caretakers…

As mom watches over them from the first moments…

And God does his miraculous work making sure there's 10 fingers and 10 toes.

Then…They are entrusted to us…

As God sent them here…

And they came from light…

And they are light.

To us…

For us.

We should learn from them.

It is all there…in their eyes.

Just look.

The innocent dependence…

Trust…

Purity and joy…

Simplicity…goodness.

Playfulness…

All the hope there ever was…

And nothing but love.

See it?

We need to be more like them.

Simpler…

More playful…

More trusting…

More loving…

And more dependent.

And just as they depend on us…

We depend on our Father in Heaven.

Learn from them.

Find what you need there.

In A Baby's eyes.

The Lesson of the Day.

A Note to Jessica

I am just leaving the hospital.

Nice discussion this morning.

Even though you have grown into this incredibly wonderful, professional woman, and you've grown very secure in many ways…you are only human and we sometimes can be frail. God, and our relationships, are there for us in those times. We are here to watch over each other.

We put love on everything. We pour it on…

And surrender to each other… In our honesty…

Our frailty…

Our human weaknesses…

And our tears…

With our triumphs…and with the lessons and opportunities from the other stuff. You are becoming more whole…transforming…and you are more like God from it. I'm glad you have become vulnerable…as that is one of the secrets of love.

But…Love is always a little risky.

It's also worth the risk.

Always love.

I have learned a lot from you and we have helped each other grow.

I love you very much.

Always,

Daddy

Used with Jessica's permission.

A Walk in the Woods

Good Morning, Brothers and Sisters.

"Are your hearts tender and compassionate? Then make me truly happy by agreeing with each other, loving one another, and working together with one mind and purpose. Don't be selfish...be humble...thinking of others as better than yourself. Don't look out only for your own interests, but take an interest in others also." Philippians 2:1-4

"Light shines in the darkness for the Godly. They are generous, compassionate, and righteous. Good comes to those who lend generously...and conduct their business fairly. Such people will not be overcome by evil." Psalm 112:4-6

"Don't just be concerned with your own good, but with the good of others." 1 Corinthians 10:24

Let's take a walk...a walk in the woods.

Way back in the day...during the Cold War...President Ronald Reagan and USSR General Secretary Leonid Brezhnev had a summit. It was 1982...Geneva, Switzerland...and the topic was nuclear arms reduction.

One of Reagan's chief negotiators, and a lead negotiator from the Soviet Union, outlined the framework for an agreement during a friendly stroll. They walked together into the woods around Geneva. They sat down on a log and talked. They got to know each other deeply...personally...and together they sketched out an agreement that was felt to be quite brilliant for the time.

Although discussions between Reagan and Brezhnev failed, a path was laid for agreements later made in Iceland between Reagan and Mikhail Gorbachev. That friendly stroll became part of history…

And it has a name.

I studied under an instructor who had been on Reagan's negotiating team. His class was about leadership, negotiation, and conflict resolution.

He called the class "A Walk in the Woods."

So…Lets take a walk.

We will get to know each other and what each holds valuable and important… Wives, children, jobs and prosperity, safety and security, and others, hopefully achieving an intimate knowledge and understanding of the other. As we walk…and talk…we find that we agree on most things.

We find that we are much more alike than different. We also find that we have some differences.

With our new-found knowledge and understanding of the other, we are able to reframe some of our needs in a give-and-take fashion achieving a mutually beneficial solution.

It's Historic… And Biblical.

There's only us.

Let's take a walk…a walk in the woods.

The Lesson of the Day.

All Men are Created Equal

Good Morning, Brothers and Sisters.

"My dear brothers and sisters, how can you claim to have faith in our Lord Jesus Christ if you favor some people over others?" James 2:1

"For there is no distinction between Jew and Greek…for the same Lord is Lord of all, bestowing his riches on all those who call on Him." Romans 10:12

"Then Peter replied: I see very clearly that God shows no favoritism." Acts 10:34

"So now I am giving you a new command: Love each other just as I have loved you. Your love for one another will prove to the world that you are my followers." John 13:34

"We hold these truths to be self-evident, that all men are created equal, that they are endowed by their Creator with certain unalienable Rights, that among these are Life, Liberty and the pursuit of Happiness." US Declaration of Independence.

All Men are Created Equal…

And have certain rights given by their Creator.

Five men were tasked with drafting a document regarding the American colonies separation from England.

It was the Second Continental Congress, the summer of 1776, in Philadelphia. The men were Thomas Jefferson, John Adams, Benjamin Franklin, Robert Livingston, and Roger Sherman.

Jefferson was the principle author of the Document.

Thomas Jefferson was a man who called himself a Christian: "…Following the simple teachings of Jesus Christ…" He felt that it was each man's duty to follow those teachings as outlined in the Gospels, and that no church or religion need interpret Christ's teachings for the individual. He also felt that the problems in England, and Europe in general, were due to tyrannical governments dictating rights as they saw fit to the people.

So why is it that we can't get this straight after all these years?

It seems so simple.

"…all men are created equal…"

It doesn't say straight or gay men, white or black men…it says all men.

"…they are endowed by their creator with certain unalienable rights…"

"…God shows no favoritism…"

Should it not be clear that all should have the same rights?

Should it not be clear that protections afforded to one class need be afforded to all?

That's a biblical principle…

And it's fundamental to our founding fathers, their thinking, and the document they wrote.

All men are created equal…

And they have rights given by their creator.

Let's get this simple stuff straight.

There is only us.

The Lesson of the Day.

12

At What Cost

Good Morning, Brothers and Sisters.

"Whoever desires to come after me let him deny himself and take up his cross and follow me. For whoever desires to save his life will lose it, and whoever loses his life for my sake will save it. For what will it profit a man if he gains the whole world and loses his soul?" Mark 8: 35,36

"Do not lay up for yourselves treasures on earth, where moth and rust destroy and where thieves steal. But lay up for yourselves treasures in heaven…For where your treasure is, there your heart will be also." Matthew 6:19-21

"…Go and sell all of your possessions and give the money to the poor…I tell you the truth, it is very hard for a rich person to enter the kingdom of heaven…It is easier for a camel to pass through the eye of a needle than it is for a rich man to enter the kingdom of God." Matthew 19:21, 23-24

What are you willing to pay to follow Jesus?

We have been asked to "…hunger and thirst after righteousness…"

"…To be merciful and forgiving…"

Not to forgive seven times, but "…seventy times seven…"

To be peacemakers.

If someone hurts you…bear it as best you can…for the sake of peace.

Give what you have to the poor.

Be kind and loving and compassionate…

be transformed…

Be more like Christ...

To love one another and bear good fruit…

And to seek first the Kingdom of God.

We all have a lot going on in this world.

And what is the price of following Jesus?

Everything.

Abraham was asked to sacrifice his son… The son he had waited so long for. Abraham knew his reward was in Heaven.

What are you willing to pay?

The Lesson of the Day.

Character

Good Morning, Brothers and Sisters.

"We rejoice in our sufferings, knowing that suffering produces endurance, and endurance produces character, and character produces hope, confident hope in salvation, because God's love has been poured into our hearts through the Holy Spirit who has been given to us." Romans 5:3-5

"Finally, brothers and sisters, fix your thoughts on whatever is true and honorable, whatever is right, whatever is pure, whatever is lovely, whatever is admirable. Think about these things that are excellent and worthy of praise." Philippians 4:8

"Put on then, as God's chosen ones, holy and beloved, compassionate hearts, kindness, humility, gentleness, and patience, bearing with one another and forgiving each other as the Lord has forgiven you. And above all these put on love, which binds everything together in perfect harmony." Colossians 3:12-14

"Consider it an opportunity when you meet trials of various kinds, for you know that the testing of your faith produces endurance. And let your endurance have its full effect, that you may be perfect and complete, lacking in nothing." James 1:2-4

Character

It is more important than any of our worldly accomplishments.

It speaks to the way we walk through the journey…

How we handle ourselves… And how we treat others.

How we handle adversity…and success.

Good character develops with experiencing the ebb and flow of life…

And watching others…and how they go about it.

Our role models teach us about good character…

It comes from deep inside…

From your soul…

Where goodness and God reside.

And it is what others will remember after we go.

Good character handles its successes with humility…

And its trials with resilience and courage.

It recognizes the needs of others and does its best to help them with empathy and compassion.

It manages its affairs with honesty and integrity…

And with a good moral compass.

Good character recognizes right and wrong…

It is disciplined, patient, and gentle.

Good character is perfect and complete…

And more important than any worldly accomplishment.

Good character puts Love on everything.

Character.

The Lesson of the Day.

Circle the Wagons

Good Morning, Brothers and Sisters.

"Carry one another's burdens; in this way you will fulfill the law of Christ." Galatians 6:2

"And let us watch out for one another to provoke love and good works." Hebrews 10:24

"Love each other as brothers and sisters, and take delight in caring for each other." Romans 12:10

Circle the Wagons.

The old west was a dangerous place…and circling the wagons protected the group…

The group, and those in the group, were safer that way.

And just as one player on a baseball team cannot go it alone, neither can we. We were meant to be in a community, in a team of individuals.

Back when cave men and saber-toothed tigers were walking around, community meant survival…

It meant provisions and protection…

We are hard wired for it.

Many experts believe that the grave reactions we have to the death of a loved one, divorce, breakup, or other major life event is from this basic instinct.

It is about life and death…

Survival or not.

That visceral, pit of your stomach, I have a headache and I feel like I'm going to die…is from these instincts.

We feel like we might really die…

And in the days of the caveman, one going it alone often did die.

So when something big happens…

We Circle the Wagons.

We care for each other.

We watch over each other.

We feed each other and bring the water.

We sit with each other and talk, and we cry…

Together.

We do whatever is necessary…

Until they can walk again.

And as they walk, we continue to walk together…

In brotherhood…in community…

As the journey is fraught with twists and turns.

We watch over each other and care for each other…

Always.

Circle the Wagons.

The Lesson of the day.

Control Your Thoughts

Good Morning, Brothers and Sisters.

"And now, dear brothers and sisters, one final thing. Fix your thoughts on what is true, and honorable and right, and pure, and lovely, and admirable. Think about things that are excellent and worthy of praise. Keep putting into practice all you learned and received from me…everything you heard from me and saw me doing. Then the God of peace will be with you." Philippians 4: 8-9

It all starts with a thought.

Every work of goodness and love.

Every act of generosity and service.

Every relationship and family.

All good things.

Every fear.

Every self-doubt.

Every self-destructive act.

And all bad things.

Everything…starts with a thought.

Thoughts are not real.

They are only thoughts.

When we act them out, they become real enough…

Sometimes too real… "What have I done?"

So…Paul advises that we control our thoughts.

We must be discerning about them and know where they come from.

The enemy often works only in our head…

In our thoughts.

"I am not worthy or strong enough."

"I'm not pretty enough."

"I don't deserve to be loved."

"Do you know what a mess I have made of things?"

Can we identify those thoughts not coming from God and eliminate them?

Can we ask ourselves: "Is that something a loving God might say to me?"

God loves you.

You are valuable and important to Him.

You are his Masterpiece.

Any thought otherwise does not come from Him.

It all starts with a thought.

Let God and his Holy Spirit control your thoughts.

The Lesson of the Day.

Crushed

Good Morning, Brothers and Sisters.

"And we know that God causes everything to work together for the good of those who love Him and are called according to His purpose for them." Romans 8:28

"Why am I so discouraged? Why is my heart so sad? I will put my hope in God and I will praise Him again…my savior and my God." Psalm 42:11

"Consider it pure joy, my brothers and sisters, whenever you face trials of many kinds as you know that the testing of faith produces perseverance. Let perseverance finish its work so that you may mature and complete…not lacking anything." James 1:2-4

"A man's spirit will endure sickness…but a crushed spirit who can bear?" Proverbs 18:14

"At times what my father allows and what I allow for the growth of my sheep can be crushing." Jesus to Thomas…The Chosen.

Crushed.

I have been a member of a great church in San Diego for about 20 years. It is a holy place…a place of God…and He is there. I am part of the Friday night bunch. The Friday night service is smaller, much more personal and cozy, and a little different from the Sunday services. We start with prayer. Often we pray over people for the stuff they bring there…the crazy stuff of life. Often, the service is a testing ground for message pieces that, if they don't go over well, won't make the cut for Sunday.

We laugh a lot.

But…sometimes…things are crushing.

A few weeks ago we prayed for a middle aged couple who had suffered a loss. The story went something like this: Their daughter, who was in her late twenties, was pregnant with twins. She had made it to her mid-30 weeks of pregnancy and went into labor. She had just made it to the hospital and staff was considering caesarean section as the babies were not in the right position. There was a sudden emergency…

A sudden, bad emergency.

Both babies died.

And mom died.

Crushed.

Really, really crushed.

In my 30-something years in medicine I have never seen that happen.

A husband and father-to-be, with all the joyous anticipation of the moment before…loses his babies…and his wife…

In just a moment.

Grand-mom and Grand-pop lost their grandchildren…and their daughter…in just a moment.

There are no words.

We will never understand why…not on this side of heaven.

Only prayer and time…

Lots of prayer and time.

Crushed.

There is a lesson there somewhere…

The Bible verses…that we are tested to be made stronger and more resilient and more perfect.

Faith, Prayer, and time.

And be ready…

Tell those important to you that you love them.

Do that today.

There's not unlimited time… And things change quickly.

Maybe those are the lessons.

Do Not Be Afraid

Good Morning Brothers and Sisters.

Do not be afraid.

These words are used in the Bible a lot. Some folks say it is used at least once for every day of the year. I recall that every time an angel appeared to someone the first words said were "Do not be afraid."

The angel Gabriel appeared to a young teenage girl named Mary to tell her that she had found favor with God and that she would bear a son, conceived of the Holy Spirit, who would be known as the Son of God. His first words to Mary were "Do not be afraid."

How many times do we sabotage ourselves with thoughts of fear…all the different ways that something will never work out…all the things that might happen…there will never be enough money…I must have some terrible disease…I will never get that job.

Jesus assures us that He is always watching over us, guiding our every step, and that there is nothing to fear.

We only need to believe.

"I have told you these things, so that in me you may have peace. In the world you will have trouble. But take heart…I have overcome the world." John 16:33

"Fear not for I am with you. Be not dismayed for I am your God. I will strengthen you and help you. I will uphold you with my righteous right hand" Isaiah 41:10

So he protects us and is with us in every step.

In our troubles we are drawn closer and more dependent on Him.

He is preparing us for something greater.

Believe…and be strong.

He is watching over all of it.

Take one step and live one moment at a time.

Do not be afraid.

The Lesson of the Day.

Do Not Judge

Good Morning, Brothers and Sisters.

"Do not judge so that you won't be judged. With the judgment you use you will be judged and with the measure you use it will be measured to you. But don't you notice the log in your own eye? Or can you say to your brother: Let me take the spec out of your eye and look there's a log in my own eye? Hypocrite! First, take the log out of your own eye then you'll see clearly to take the spec out of your brother's eye." Matthew 7:1-5

It is difficult for me to understand why this lesson is so difficult.

How is it so easy to point at another's faults?

A look in the mirror might reveal the log in your own eye.

I think our culture needs a big dose of self-reflection.

What is the stuff we're putting out there?

Is it goodness and love…or something else?

Is it light…or darkness?

How many different ways can we divide ourselves?

Can we ever get out of our own way?

Not much has changed in a few thousand years.

It only changes if we change it.

Take it upon yourself to be that change.

Be a light in a dark place.

Embrace love and goodness, kindness and empathy…

Patience and tolerance.

Talk to each other and do your best to understand.

Look in the mirror first…And…

Do Not Judge.

The Lesson of the Day.

Don't Let Love Die

Good Morning, Brothers and Sisters.

"Love never dies a natural death. It dies because we don't know how to replenish it. It dies of blindness and errors and betrayals. It dies of illness and wounds; it dies of weariness, of witherings, and of tarnishings." -Anais Nin-

God is Love.

Find Him.

Open the door.

He stands there waiting for you.

He will come in and fill you with his love.

Bathe in it.

Let it fill you.

Then…His love will flow through you…

As you are the branches of His vine.

Give it away continuously and freely.

Stay connected to Him...to the source of love.

Don't Let Love Die.

The Lesson of the Day.

Don't Worry About Tomorrow

Good Morning, Brothers and Sisters.

I wasn't quite sure what I was going to write this morning.

I was sitting out back as I usually do and I looked up, and I saw a little bird sitting on top of the house looking about.

Inspiration.

I like to get up in the morning and sit out back with Marty and Jenny. The day is just beginning. I have coffee. Coffee makes it easy too think, read, and pray. Sometimes it's sunny, sometimes overcast, sometimes cold, but often not. One thing it always is…it's full of inspiration.

Life is all around.

The grass is a beautiful deep green. The plants are blossoming. The birds are singing, and just now the sun is creeping around the side of the house.

God's beautiful creation.

And, Jenny is barking at one of the birds.

I am lucky every day to be able to do this.

Blessed is probably a better word.

So today remember gratitude.

Try to not worry.

Remember love and simple blessings.

Remember that it doesn't take a lot and that right now your Father in heaven loves you and you have everything that you need.

"That is why I tell you not to worry. Don't worry about having enough food or drink or enough clothes to wear. Isn't life more important than food, and your body more important than clothing? Look at the birds. They don't plant or harvest or store food. And your heavenly Father feeds them and watches after them. And aren't you far more valuable to Him than they are?" Mathew 6: 25, 26

The Lesson of the Day.

Einstein and Love

Good Morning, Brothers and Sisters.

When I proposed the theory of relativity, very few understood me, and what I will reveal now, to transmit to mankind, will also collide with the misunderstanding and prejudice in the world.

I ask you to guard the letters as long as necessary, years, decades, until society is advanced enough to accept what I will explain below.

There is an extremely powerful force that, so far, science has not found a formal explanation to. It is a force that includes and governs all others, and is even behind any phenomenon operating in the universe and has not yet been identified by us. This universal force is LOVE.

When scientists looked for a unified theory of the universe they forgot the most powerful unseen force.

Love is Light, that enlightens those who give and receive it.

Love is gravity, because it makes people feel attracted to each other.

Love is power, because it multiplies the best we have, and allows humanity not to be extinguished in their blind selfishness.

Love unfolds and reveals.

For love we live and die.

Love is God and God is Love.

This force explains everything and gives meaning to life. This is the variable that we have ignored for too long, maybe because we are afraid of love because it is the only energy in the universe that man has not learned to drive at will.

To give visibility to love, I made a simple substitution in my most famous equation. If instead of E = mc2, we accept that the energy to heal the world can be obtained through love multiplied by the speed of light squared, we arrive at the conclusion that love is the most powerful force there is, because it has no limits.

After the failure of humanity in the use and control of the other forces of the universe that have turned against us, it is urgent that we nourish ourselves with another kind of energy.

If we want our species to survive, if we are to find meaning in life, if we want to save the world and every sentient being that inhabits it, love is the one and only answer.

Perhaps we are not yet ready to make a bomb of love, a device powerful enough to entirely destroy the hate, selfishness and greed that devastate the planet.

However, each individual carries within them a small but powerful generator of love whose energy is waiting to be released.

When we learn to give and receive this universal energy, dear Lieserl, we will have affirmed that love conquers all, and is able to transcend everything and anything, because love is the quintessence of life.

I deeply regret not having been able to express what is in my heart, which has quietly beaten for you all my life. Maybe it's too late to apologize, but as time is relative, I need to tell you that I love you and thanks to you I have reached the ultimate answer.

Your father, Albert Einstein

There is controversy about this letter and some experts believe it was not written by Einstein himself. There are also many questions, and not much known, about his first daughter Lieserl.

I chose to use this letter here as it, in my opinion, accurately represents the universal importance of love. It also, again in my opinion, represents the vast intersection between science and faith.

The Lesson of the Day.

Emotional Maturity

Good Morning, Brothers and Sisters.

"I have said these things to you, that in me you may have peace. In the world you will have tribulation. But take heart; I have overcome the world." John 16:33

"And the Holy Spirit helps us in our weakness." Romans 8:26

"You will keep in perfect peace all who trust in you, all whose thoughts are fixed on you." Romans 26:3

"Don't worry about anything; instead pray about everything. Tell God what you need and thank Him for all He has done. Then you will experience God's peace, which exceeds anything we can understand. His peace will guard your hearts and minds as you live in Christ Jesus." Philippians 4:6

Emotional Maturity.

Life will challenge you every day.

With things you have seen before...

Often something new...

Those challenges come in our relationships...

At home with our spouses and children...those closest to us...

Or at work...our bosses...our professional colleagues.

They can be financial challenges...

Or challenges with our health.

We can even be tested by another driver on the highway.

Our emotions often tell it all...

Calm, objective, analytical, sensible.

Anxious, flustered, emotional, reactive.

Calm, predictable behavior lends itself to the same in those around you.

A leader with an emotional, reactive approach will also soon see that in others.

I once needed to discuss something with my boss and a colleague advised: "Don't go in there today."

Which person will those around you find behind the door?

The Bible is full of Christ's instructions here.

As we let the Holy Spirit transform us we embrace God's love and goodness.

We become more tolerant and patient.

We listen more…as we are quiet enough to do so.

We are more flexible…

And more resilient.

We understand that He has overcome the world…and everything in it.

Our God is a God of order, tranquility, and peacefullness.

He is not a God of confusion, calamity, and chaos.

We can depend on Him.

As we grow closer to Him, and more like Him, we become more calm, more peaceful…

Our thoughts become more orderly…

And our behavior more predictable.

We also become more reliable…more dependable.

As we practice His instructions the challenges become less severe…

And life's ebb and flow becomes less so…

As we never move far from the center.

You see…those around you need to know who they will find there.

Be transformed.

Emotional Maturity.

The Lesson of the Day.

Even John the Baptist Doubted

Good Morning, Brothers and Sisters.

"Sarah was listening to the conversation from the tent. Abraham and Sarah were very old by this time and Sarah was long past the age of having children. So she laughed silently to herself and said: How could a worn out woman like me enjoy such a pleasure especially when my husband is also so old?" Genesis 18:10-12

"When John, who was in prison, heard about the deeds of the messiah, he sent his followers to ask Him: Are you the one who is to come, or should we expect someone else?" Matthew 11:2,3

"So John agreed to Baptize Him. After His baptism, as Jesus came up out of the water, the heavens were opened and He saw the Spirit of God descending like a dove and settling upon Him. And a voice from heaven said: This is my dearly loved son…who brings me great joy." Matthew 3:15-16

Even John the Baptist doubted.

John the Baptist was Jesus' cousin and they were born only months apart. We are told that when Mary, pregnant with Jesus, went to see her cousin Elizabeth, pregnant with John, the baby in Elizabeth's womb leaped with joy.

So John knew Jesus even before he was born

John and Jesus were very close.

He was there from the first moments.

They grew up together.

He saw as a young Jesus taught with knowledge far beyond his years.

John heard what The Father spoke at the time of Jesus Baptism.

And still he had doubt.

Abraham and Sarah were close to God.

When they were told that Sarah would bear a son at their advanced age…They had doubt.

And so it is with our human nature.

How is it that we can understand the almighty?

He created us…and He created the universe.

He is the Master of all.

How is it that we can understand an all-powerful, all-knowing and loving God?

He was present before time existed…

And He knew us then…

He knows all about us now…our thoughts, our concerns, our needs, and our secrets.

And He will be forever…long after the sun and the stars stop shining.

A God that has defeated even death.

He can change any of it with a thought.

How is it that we understand any of that?

I am not sure there is understanding…only faith.

As we look closer…He reveals Himself to us through prayer and through His word.

We see Him all about us in His wonderful creation.

But understanding is elusive.

And it is only by faith and trust, that we find some sense of that…

A sense of the infinite, the all-knowing, and the all-powerful creator of all.

We Believe…

And we Pray…

And we trust and have faith.

Yet…still…

We all have times of doubt…

And we do our best to understand…knowing that…

Even John the Baptist had Some Doubt.

The Lesson of the Day.

Fertile Soil

Good Morning, Brothers and Sisters.

"Later that same day Jesus left the house and sat beside the lake. A large crowd soon gathered around him, so he got into a boat. There he sat and taught as the people stood on the shore. He told many stories in the form of parables…such as this one:

A farmer went out to plant some seeds. As he scattered them across the fields some seeds fell on a footpath and the birds came and ate them. Other seeds fell on shallow soil with underlying rock. The seeds sprouted quickly but the plants soon withered and died as they didn't have deep roots. Other seeds fell among the thorns that grew up and choked the tender plants. Still other seeds fell on fertile soil and yielded thirty, sixty, and perhaps one-hundred times that which was planted. Anyone with ears to hear should listen and understand." Matthew 13:1-9

"I am the the true grapevine, and my Father is the Gardner. He cuts off every branch of mine that doesn't produce fruit, and He prunes the branches that do bear fruit, so they will produce even more."
John 15:1-2

"I am the vine and you are the branches. Those who remain in me, and I in them, will produce much fruit." John 15:5

Fertile Soil.

I am sitting here at a beautiful winery near my house.

The beauty of God's creation always inspires me. I find that the Word comes alive in these places.

As I quiet and calm myself…and listen…

I am inspired.

I see this scripture all about me.

The winemaker must first prepare the soil…test it…and if it is not quite right then he must amend it…fertilize it, and adjust things as they should be. He will choose the perfect hill side, the perfect sunlight and drainage…and when things are just right he will carefully plant the grape's seeds in just the right place.

And so it is with us.

He prepared the way just for us.

He gave us just the right parents at just the right time.

Then He gave us Life.

And He feeds us with His love…

And He teaches us…

And He watches us grow.

And when we are ready…

He plants His seeds in us.

And we continue to grow, as we are now transformed…

And we grow…

And we become ready.

To take the Good News to the World…

And bear much fruit.

Fertile soil.

The Lesson of the Day.

Find God's Glory All Around You

Good Morning, Brothers and Sisters.

"And God looked over all he had made and saw that it was very good. And evening past and morning came. The sixth day." Genesis 1:31

Find God's glory all around you.

Look carefully…

With gratitude.

The Lesson of the Day.

Fishers of Men

Good Morning, Brothers and Sisters.

"Go into all the world and preach the gospel to everyone."
Mark 16:15

"Go and make disciples of all nations. Baptize them in the name of the Father and the Son and the Holy Spirit. Teach them to obey everything I have commanded you. I am with you always, even to the end of the age." Matthew 28:19, 20

"Come follow me and I will make you fishers of men."
Matthew 4:19

It all started with a carpenter from Galilee who had a different message…a message of love. He had 11 guys, they only counted the men in those days, and he told them to take His message out to the world.

He has over 2 billion followers today…

And still more…meeting in secret for fear of governments around the world.

I was in Israel a few years ago. I was standing there with my church group and our Pastor was talking about this. He mentioned that San Diego was about halfway around the world from where we stood…as far as any place could be.

So…Look what happened…

A carpenter…

A few guys…

And a message of love.

He was more influential than any human being.

He was the Son of Man.

So…never underestimate the influence you may have on people around you.

Always smile.

Always be gracious and good and kind.

Always be tolerant and respectful…

With Love…lots of it.

Take the Good News to the world…your little part of it anyway.

Follow Him and cast your net…

Be Fishers of Men.

The Lesson of the Day.

Flashlight

Good Morning, Brothers and Sisters.

"Give to the one who asks you and do not turn away from the one who wants to borrow from you." Matthew 5:42

"Do to others as you would have them do unto you." Luke 6:31

"Then Peter came to Jesus and asked: Lord, if my brother continues to sin against me how many times should I forgive him? Seven times? And Jesus replied: No, not seven times…But seventy times seven." Matthew 18:21, 22

A friend of mine's pastor wrote this sometime ago:

"When a flashlight grows dim or quits working, you don't throw it away, you change the batteries.

When a person messes up and finds themselves in a dark place, do you cast them aside? Of course not…you help them change their batteries. Some need AA… Attention and Affection; Some need AAA…Attention, Affection and Acceptance; Some need C…Compassion; Some need D…Direction. And if they still don't seem to shine… simply sit with them and quietly share your light."

Nicely said.

A Father had a celebration when his lost son returned. He gave him a beautiful robe and a ring…and they celebrated his son's return.

And so it is with our Father in heaven.

The Lesson of the Day.

For Everything There is a Season

Good Morning, Brothers and Sisters.

"For everything there is a season, a time for every activity under heaven. A time to be born and a time to die. A time to plant and a time to harvest. A time to kill and a time to heal. A time to tear down and a time to build up. A time to cry and a time to laugh. A time to grieve and a time to dance. A time to scatter stones and a time to gather stones. A time to embrace and a time to turn away. A time to search and a time to quit searching. A time to keep and a time to throw away. A time to tear and a time to mend. A time to be quiet and a time to speak. A time to love and a time to hate. A time for war and a time for peace." Ecclesiastes 3: 1-8

This well-known passage was written by King Solomon, one of the wisest of the prophets.

All of us understand of what Solomon speaks…

The Seasons of Life.

There are times of incredible joy:

The birth of a child.

A beautiful, enduring marriage.

Working or playing with incredible teammates.

Achieving goals.

Giving and receiving love.

A job very well done.

And then times of incredible pain:

The end of a marriage.

A close friend walks away.

The death of a loved one.

The loss of an important job.

The feeling that love is nowhere around.

In all of it, we are asked to remember that nothing can separate us from God and His love.

He is always there…in the great stuff…and the other stuff…

In all of the seasons.

Right with us…next to us.

He asks us to sing, to celebrate and clap our hands with the angels…in that season.

He comforts us…He strengthens us, He supports and protects us…in that season.

He is always there…

In Every Season.

The Lesson of the Day.

Forgiveness

Good Morning, Brothers and Sisters.

"But when you are praying, first forgive anyone you are holding a grudge against, so that your Father in heaven will forgive your sins as well." Mark 11:25

"Then Peter came up and said to him: Lord, how often Should I forgive someone who sins against me? Seven times? And Jesus replied: No, not seven times, but seventy times seven."
Matthew 18:21-22

"Make allowance for each other's faults, and forgive anyone who offends you. Remember that the Lord forgave you, so you must forgive others…And let the peace that comes from Christ rule in your heart." Colossians 4:13,15

"And Jesus said: Father, forgive them, for they don't know what they are doing." Luke 23:34

Forgiveness

We are commanded to forgive…

To forgive when it is hardest to forgive…

As Christ gave forgiveness with His last words on the cross.

And Paul says…

Let forgiveness restore the peace of Christ in your heart.

Forgiveness will restore you...

And free you…

From the burdens of not forgiving…

From the anger and pain of not forgiving.

Forgiving will heal you…

And help you move forward.

And as God has been merciful and forgiving…

So should we.

And we give love with our forgiveness…

Often to those most difficult to love and forgive.

"…And forgive us our trespasses, as we forgive those who trespass against us…"

As Jesus taught us to pray, He asked us to forgive…

To forgive…as we bring heaven to earth.

With Christ's peace in your heart…

Give forgiveness.

Relieve yourself of the burdens.

Let yourself be restored…

With love…

And with peace.

Forgiveness.

The Lesson of the Day.

Fourth of July

Good Morning, Brothers and Sisters.

Happy Fourth of July to all.

I always have enjoyed this holiday.

When I was young, it typically meant a baseball game or two, lots of time with the family, cooking out on the grill, and of course…fireworks.

Common sense suggests that this country should have never come to be.

At the time the British Army and Navy were the best the world had ever seen. The Bible has many stories about an underdog winning a battle against overwhelming odds.

Only by God's grace.

I believe this country was ordained by God.

Here is a little of what our founding fathers say about our faith and being a good citizen.

"While we are zealously performing the duties of good citizens and soldiers…we certainly should not be inattentive of the duties given to us by God. It should be our highest duty to add to our character as a Christian." George Washington

"Suppose a nation should take the Bible as their own law book and every member should regulate his conduct by the precepts there in. Every member would be regulated in his conscience to justice, kindness, and charity toward his fellow man…And piety, love, and reverence toward Almighty God. What a utopia and paradise this would be." John Adams

"Resistance to tyranny becomes the Christian and social duty of each individual…notably to defend those rights that heaven has given us and no man ought take away." John Hancock

"Here is my creed. I believe in one God, the creator of the universe. That he governs it by his providence and ought to be worshiped." Benjamin Franklin.

Timeless words…

Only by the grace of God.

Happy Fourth of July.

The Lesson of the Day

Generosity

Good Morning, Brothers and Sisters.

"The point is this: whoever sows sparingly will also reap sparingly, and whoever sows bountifully will also reap bountifully." 2 Corinthians 9:6

"Give and it will be given to you. For with the measure you use…it will also be measured back to you." Luke 6:38

"Whoever brings blessings will be enriched and one who waters will himself be watered." Proverbs 11:25

Generosity.

Generosity is Love in action.

We don't have to give…

We choose to give…

We get to give.

We get to participate.

You see...when we give of ourselves we are participating in God's work.

We give of our resources...our time...our talents...and the dollars we have been blessed with.

Sometimes it is just listening as a friend opens up. Sometimes it is just offering to sit there with them. No one should cry alone.

Sometimes it looks different. I work with a Foundation established by some ER docs and we do homeless clinics at local shelters. The need is big.

It is also supporting the work of the church...the good work of the church...Missions, food banks, clothing, and casting a bigger net...

We are Fishers of Men... aren't we?

We choose to give to God's work.

"As you do to the least of your brothers, you also do to me."

The need is big.

Generosity…

Love in action.

The Lesson of the Day.

God Has You Where He Wants You.

Good Morning, Brothers and Sisters.

"Now God has us where he wants us, with all the time in the world, and He will next shower grace and kindness upon us through Jesus Christ...All we need do is trust Him enough to let Him do it." Ephesians 2:7

"From one man He created all the Earth. He decided beforehand when they should rise and fall, and he determined their boundaries." Acts 17:26

"And don't be wishing you were someplace else or with someone else. Where you are right now is God's place for you. Live and love and obey right here." 1 Corinthians 7:17

You are right where He wants you...

In the exact spot.

The Creator of the Universe makes no mistakes.

You arrived at the intended time...on the exact day, in the exact year, in the exact place...that He intended.

He knew you even before the heavens were made.

He knew all of your steps...

And all of your missteps.

There is a great order to all of it...

A plan...

And the plan is unfolding in front of you in the moment.

Even in the pain of the trials, He is working…working behind the scenes.

He is preparing you, and the people and things necessary, for the next and magnificent part of your story.

It is on its way…

And it is already yours.

It is already written in His book.

Trust Him.

Pray with gratitude as He reveals it to you.

He has you right where he wants you.

The Lesson of the Day.

On Love

Good Morning, Brothers and Sisters.

I didn't do much writing over the weekend as some things happened. They were awful. My friend and her family wound up in the ER with her elderly mom who had fallen. I joined them there. Among the kaos of the ER, I was lucky enough to witness love in abundance between her, her family, and their mom.

It was love…and it was there in abundance.

We can't choose the things that come our way and we can only choose what we do with them. I was fortunate enough to find love…and see love…there.

I came across this Short piece as I was reading last night.

Enjoy your family, in love, today.

And enjoy as Khalil Gibran speaks of love:

"On Love"

Love has no other desire but to fulfill itself.

But if you love and must needs have desires, let these be your desires:

To melt and be like a running brook that sings its melody to the night.

To know the pain of too much tenderness.

To be wounded by your own understanding of love;

And to bleed willingly and joyfully.

To wake at dawn with a winged heart and give thanks for another day of loving;

To rest at the noon hour and meditate love's ecstasy;

To return home at eventide with gratitude.

And then to sleep with a prayer for the beloved in your heart and a song of praise upon your lips.

Kahlil Gibran, "The Prophet"

The Lesson of the Day.

Grace

Good Morning, Brothers and Sisters.

"We are saved by grace as a gift, through the redemption that is Jesus Christ. " Romans 3:24

"Many have died from one man's trespass. Many more have been saved by the free gift of grace through Christ Jesus ..." Romans 5:15

"My grace is sufficient for you, for my power is made perfect in weakness." 2 Corinthians 12:9

Only by the Grace of God.

His grace touches every part of our lives.

He is a loving and a grace-full God.

That is how He is.

He is our Father. He wants to bless his children with his goodness, His gifts, and with His grace-full nature.

He loves us and is good to us even when we go astray…

Even when we don't deserve his blessing and grace.

You see…His Grace is free…

And His grace is limitless.

His grace is what keeps us strong in times of trial.

His grace gives us peace when it's not peaceful.

It gives us the birds that sing…

And a goodnight's sleep.

Our work.

And our families.

Puppies and coffee.

Beautiful mornings and evenings.

And innumerable chances to return to him when we go astray.

Everything we need…

Only by the Grace of God.

The Lesson of the Day.

Gratitude

Good Morning, Brothers and Sisters.

"Give thanks in all circumstances; for this is the will of God in Christ Jesus for you." 1 Thessalonians 5:18

"Give thanks to the Lord, for he is good. His love endures forever." Psalm 136:1

"All this is for your benefit, so that the grace that is reaching more and more people may cause thanksgiving to overflow to the glory of God." 2 Corinthians 4:15

"Thanks be to God for his incredible gift." 2 Corinthians 9:15

Gratitude.

Be thankful.

Every good and perfect gift is from above.

He created all of this for us…

For life in abundance.

Be thankful…

For all of it…

The moon and the stars and the planets…

And a cool and crisp, clear night to see them.

The bluest of skies…the birds and their songs…

For the oceans and the rivers…And all of the creatures there.

The mountains and forests…And the low valleys.

For the whitest-of-white snow…and the rain that cools a summer's afternoon. And the infinite colors of the rainbow that follows.

Nature…His creation…The beauty, glory, and awe in all of it.

Our parents and those who influenced us.

Our families…our children.

Our jobs…how we give back…a purpose for being here.

Laughter…

Colorado, my precious river, and the Aspens.

Baseball.

My stupid brothers…

Health…

Hope…

This moment…and the next.

And the memories of yesterday's moments.

And all the smiles that they give us.

Be Thankful.

Gratitude.

The Lesson of the Day.

He Will Answer.

Good Morning, Brothers and Sisters.

"Let us hold tightly without wavering to the hope we affirm, for God can be trusted to keep his promises." Hebrews 10:23

"Remember how you remained faithful even though it meant terrible suffering." Hebrews 10:32

"Patient endurance is what you need now, so that you will continue to do God's will…Then you will receive all that He has promised." Hebrews 10:36

"In the last days God says: I will pour out my Spirit on all people. Your sons and daughters will prophesy, your young men will see visions, your old men will dream dreams." Acts 2:17

"When they had gone, an angel of the Lord appeared to Joseph in a dream. "Get up," he said, "take the child and his mother and escape to Egypt. Stay there until I tell you, for Herod is going to search for the child to kill him." Matthew 2:13

"An angel of the Lord appeared to him in a dream and said, "Joseph, Son of David, do not be afraid to take Mary home as your wife, because what is conceived in her is from the Holy Spirit." Matthew 1:20

"For God does speak—now one way, now another— though no one recognizes it. In a dream, in a vision of the night, when deep sleep falls on people as they slumber in their beds." Job 33:14,15

He Will Answer.

He is a God that keeps His promises.

Sometimes…often…we long…we wait…

For Him to speak to us…

For His guidance.

We ask Him to reveal Himself…to answer our questions…to make His will clear.

And as seasons change…sometimes there is abundance…sometimes drought.

Sometimes the sun is bright…sometimes more clouds.

And as we wait…tomorrow…the sun shines again… The drought passes…

And abundance returns…

As seasons change…in His sacred time.

He is a God of His word…

He keeps His promises.

He will answer.

The Lesson of the Day.

He's Got This

Good Morning, Brothers and Sisters.

"Let your hope make you glad. Be patient in times of trouble and never stop praying." Romans 12:12

"I will never fail you. I will never abandon you." Hebrews 13:5,6

"I will be with you always...even until the end of the age." Matthew 28:20

"I have commanded you to be strong and brave. Don't ever be afraid or discouraged… I will be there to help you wherever you go." Joshua 1:9

He's Got This

Rest easy...He has this…

Even when He is quiet.

This is the hardest thing for me…

Waiting on God.

We pray…

And we pray some more.

He asks us to fast when prayer and faith are not enough.

So we have faith, we pray, and we fast.

And often...He is still quiet.

The Israelites wandered the desert for 40 years. There were many trials...difficult trials. Some were so difficult that they thought about going back to Egypt...that being slaves was better than the desert.

So...it took a long time to get to the promised land.

I hate that.

The athlete in me wants to get it done...you know..." Just Do It!"

When I wear my doctor hat I want to fix it...

If the blood pressure is too high...bring it down. If the blood pressure is too low...bring it up.

And I'm human...waiting stinks.

Sometimes there is nothing more to do...other than pray...pray some more...and think about fasting...

And know that his plan for us is more magnificent than we might imagine...

And trust that He is working behind the scenes...aligning all the necessary pieces.

Be patient.

His timing is always perfect.

And know...

He's Got This.

The Lesson of the day.

Heartbreak

Good Morning, Brothers and Sisters.

"For my yoke is easy and my burden light." Matthew 11:30

"Consider it pure joy, my brothers and sisters, whenever you face trials of many kinds, because you know that the testing of your faith produces perseverance. Let perseverance finish its work so that you may be mature and complete…not lacking anything." James 1:2-4

"God is our refuge and strength…a very present help in times of trouble." Psalm 46:1

"Do not fear for I am with you…I will strengthen you and help you. I will uphold you with my righteous right hand." Isaiah 41:10

"Let not your hearts be troubled. Believe in God. Believe also in Me." John 14:1

Heartbreak.

There are many bible verses about how God sustains us and heals us in times of trial.

We are all the same.

We all bear the same stuff in life.

I think that one of the healing secrets is to allow ourselves to be vulnerable to each other…to share our stories…understanding that, through God, there is strength in community.

That is really hard for me.

My dad was a Marine and taught me to be tough and self-reliant. It has been my blessing…and my burden.

I am in the midst of a trial…a difficult one.

I was seeing a woman and we were very close. We were thinking about the future and started to talk about plans. I fell for her. I trusted her. I became vulnerable and I surrendered…I loved her.

One day I received a text…" Its over."

"I'm sorry?" I replied.

"It's over."

There had been no conflict, no fighting, no words…Nothing…

Nothing.

There has been minimal contact…one word answers to texts…more often no answer, no return calls.

So…lots of questions…no answers. It has been brutally painful.

Questions about what happened…

What did I do?

Questions about myself…and my self-worth…do I not deserve an explanation?

Questions about her…lots of those.

Clearly it was not what I thought.

Or maybe it was…and she became afraid.

The world became quiet in just a few moments. I saw her everywhere… reminders everywhere.

I am lucky to be surrounded by a Godly group of men who kept my head above water.

My stomach hurt…I had a headache…I couldn't eat.

I found comfort just sitting in church.

I have been reading the Bible.

I have been writing…it's therapy.

I am better.

The pain is less…but there are days.

I am growing and learning.

I think that God saved me from her.

He has given me strength and refuge.

We are all the same…

And go through the same stuff…

And why not me?

He walks with us. He strengthens us. He heals us.

He asks that we continue to walk…

And continue to love…

We learn…We grow…

And we continue to move ahead…

We forgive…and we love…

We must continue to love.

Heartbreak.

The Lesson of the Day.

His Time

Good Morning, Brothers and Sisters.

"For everything, there is a season and a time for every matter under heaven" Ecclesiastes 3:1

"He has made everything beautiful in its time." Ecclesiastes 3:1

"For still the vision awaits its appointed time…If it seems slow, wait for it; it will surely come; it will not delay." Habakkuk 2:3

"Wait patiently on the Lord. Be brave and courageous. Yes…wait patiently on the Lord." Psalm 27:14

"And let us not grow weary of doing good, for in due season we will reap, if we do not give up." Galatians 6:9

His Time.

Please quiet yourself… Calm yourself…

Be strong and courageous…

And be patient with God.

And while we wait…

Have gratitude for the things around you…

The most simple things…

The cool breeze.

The comfortable place we rest.

A hummingbird.

The coffee.

A child.

Notice it…

Notice the moment at hand.

And while we wait…

Do good deeds…

For others.

Fill their needs…

Sit with them and listen to them…talk to them.

And give more of yourself.

And while we wait…

Praise Him.

Sing to Him.

Seek Him.

Read.

Pray.

And listen.

And while you wait…

Remain quiet, calm, brave and courageous…

Be of service…

Be thankful and patient.

Everything has an appointed time…

His Time.

The Lesson of the Day.

Hope

Good Morning, Brothers and Sisters.

"For I know the plans I have for you, declares the Lord, plans for welfare and not for evil, to give you a future and a hope."
Jeremiah 29:11

"May the God of hope fill you with all joy and peace as you trust in him, so that you may overflow with hope by the power of the Holy Spirit." Romans 15:13

"Rejoice in hope, be patient in tribulation, be constant in prayer."
Romans 12:12

"As long as there is the next moment…there is hope." Mitch Albom, "The Time Keeper"

"To live without hope is to cease to live." Dostoyevsky

Hope…

Something inside of us that, when we are beaten down, compels us to look ahead and keep moving.

It's an optimistic thought.

It can be words we read, or a friend's kind and compassionate touch.

It can be hope for truth or goodness…

Or for peace…

Or for love.

We hope to stay close to God and do His work…

That's real hope.

It can be caring for another…

Or…letting someone care for us…

Restoring hope.

It is a dream that we see clearly…

A dream for light…and good fruit…

And love…

Hope pushes on until it finds those things.

A smile.

A friendly face.

Kind words.

Dependable…safe.

Hope…it is what we do when we don't see any of it.

Sometimes…only making it to the next moment…until those things find us.

Hope.

The Lesson of the Day.

I Am

Good Morning, Brothers and Sisters.

"And Moses said to God: When I come to the children of Israel and say to them that the God of your fathers has sent me to you and they ask: What is his name? What should I say to them? And God said to Moses: I Am that I Am... So say to the children of Israel that "I Am" sent you to them." Exodus 3:13-14

"And Jesus said to them...I say to you that before Abraham was, I Am." John 8:58

"Jesus fully realized what was about to happen and he asked them: Who are you looking for? Jesus the Nazarene, they replied. And Jesus said 'I am.'" John 18:4-5

I Am.

That is God's name.

That's what He called himself when Moses asked Him.

That is what Jesus called Himself when he was arrested.

It is a peculiar name.

If we look at the word "Am" it is a present tense, first person, singular form of the word "be".

So God is referring to Himself...in the first person.

"Am" is in the present tense...so that means now.

"Am" is the continuous and ongoing form of the word "Be."

"Am" is singular…only one.

So...a singular God…is now, continuous and ongoing…

One God who always was, is now, and always will be.

That's what "I Am" means.

He was there before time.

He was there before anything...when nothing existed.

He breathed life into all that we know.

He hurled the stars into the sky...He created the planets.

He created the oceans and the animals...

The sun and the moon…

And all of it.

His name is…

"I Am."

The Lesson of the Day.

I Stand at the Door and Knock

Good Morning, Brothers and Sisters.

"I stand at the door and knock. If you hear my voice and open the door I will come in and we will share a meal together as friends." Revelation 3:20

Many of you know my eldest daughter's story.

Jessica was about 12 years old when her mom and I divorced.

Both mom and I made some big mistakes and I think that Jessica was collateral damage.

In junior high and early in high school Jessica was a good kid, a good student, and a great athlete. Late in her sophomore year things began to change…she was less attentive in conversations, grades started to decline, and her athleticism was suffering. We started getting calls from the principal's office that Jessica was not in class. We talked to Jessica over and again and she told us that everyone was wrong…that she was always in class…and that no one knew what they were talking about. That trajectory continued for her. At some point, and I am not sure exactly how, we learned that she had fallen in with the wrong crowd, and that the drug and alcohol issue was now front and center.

I know that many of you have experienced this.

Jessica was in and out of rehab several times. Mom, dad, and her brother and sister suffered along with her as that darkness draws everything into it.

She was in rehab on her 18th birthday. She was released shortly thereafter and was staying at mom's until we figured out what was next. Just days later, she took mom's car and was involved in a high speed, 3 car accident on Interstate 8. She was very drunk. 3 cars were totaled. Only by the grace of God, and His Angels in the cars, no one died and there were only minor injuries.

Jessica was arrested and was facing 2 counts of felony DUI. She spent a month in jail. She doesn't remember the accident (God is good…isn't He?) and the memory of that time begins when she was being booked. Knowing that things had dramatically gone from bad to worse, she told the police that she was going to hurt herself. Taking that seriously, she was put in solitary confinement. She tells me that she was half naked and on her knees, banging her head against the wall when she said: "God…I don't even know if you are real, but if you are…I am in serious trouble and I need your help."

In an instant she told me that she felt relief…that things would be OK…but between here and there things might be a little hard.

Things were a little hard for a while…but they turned out more than OK. Jessica is now about 14 years clean and a Trauma Nurse in a Chicago ER…

She is a good, Godly girl.

God is good…and He's got this.

Open the Door.

The Lesson of the Day.

Intersection of Science and Faith

Good Morning, Brothers and Sisters.

"Many people have set out to write accounts about the events that have occurred among us. They use the eyewitness reports from the early followers. Having carefully investigated everything, I have also decided to write a careful account for you, most honorable friends, so that you can be certain of the truth of everything that has happened"

These are the first lines of the Gospel of Luke.

Luke was a physician.

Many feel that he was one of the greatest historians of the era.

Many Experts also feel that his writing style suggests that he was one of the most educated men of his time.

I'm not sure exactly why I put this in here other than to say that I am a science guy too…and only our faith brings us to believe that Christ was the son of God.

Luke says that there were many testimonials to that.

As I mention, Luke was a scientist. He wrote about Christ's life from the beginning to the end, and included most things in the middle.

Luke testifies, as do the people he spoke to, that Christ was the Messiah, the son of God.

Christ was the one who created the universe. He threw all the stars into the sky.

He created the great order that Einstein and others have attested to.

He created all of it.

Humans define our universe and everything in it with mathematical equations…the very complex equations of physics and chemistry.

Einstein also mentions that as we learn more of the order of things we understand more how God thought.

The second law of thermodynamics forbids that any system become more orderly without outside influence.

So where did all the order come from?

I guess what I'm trying to say here is that it's not either/or, science or faith. The line between the two is barely noticeable.

The intersection between science and faith is huge. You will never find a scientist that can really tell you how all of this came about. It breaks all the rules…

Unless you put God into the equation.

The Lesson of the Day.

Invest in Him

Good Morning, Brothers and sisters.

"Come close to God, and God will come close to you." James 4:8

"So faith comes from hearing…hearing the Good News of Christ." Romans 10:17

"In those days that you pray, I will listen. If you look for me with all your heart, you will find me." Jeremiah 29:12-13

"Never stop praying." 1 Thessalonians 5:17

"Before daybreak the next morning, Jesus got up and went to an isolated place to pray." Mark 1:35

Invest in Him

Nothing happens without it.

And just as you might invest in anything good… Invest in your relationship with God.

He is standing at the door… And He's Knocking.

Open the door.

My pastor says that if there is 100 steps to be taken in the relationship, Jesus will take ninety-nine…

But you must take one.

Set aside some time…

Open the door.

Visit with him and have a meal.

Talk to Him…

And listen to Him…

Just as you would with a friend.

There are lots of stories about Him…

Read the stories.

Think about the stories… And the lessons there.

Talk about the stories with your friends.

Take time…

Quiet and calm yourself…

Close your eyes and breathe deep.

Find Him in your soul…

In your quiet and calm peacefulness.

Spend time there…

And let the relationship grow.

Invest in Him.

The Lesson of the Day.

It Doesn't Change Anything

Good Morning, Brothers and Sisters.

"I am the way, the truth, and the life. No one can come to the Father except through me." John 14:6

"I tell you the truth. Anyone who believes in Me has eternal life. Yes…I am the bread of life." John 6:47-48

"So God created man in His own image. In the image of God He created them." Genesis 1:27

"For we are God's masterpiece." Ephesians 2:10

It doesn't change anything.

This trip can be full of surprises.

Some surprises are great…

Your wife comes in with a big smile and tells you that, soon, you will be a daddy.

How great is that?

And some surprises are bad…

You get a call from the doctor that there is a spot on the X-Ray.

And there are lots of surprises in between…

Broken bones.

Unexpected bills.

The car breaks down.

But…you see…none of that changes anything.

A life-long friend supported me in a recent challenge and told me: "On your best day you are a child of God. And on your worst day you are a child of God"

Every day.

And we were created in His image and likeness…

His Masterpiece.

And He is the same now….as He was before…The same as before time existed…

And He will be the same long after time has passed.

He will never change.

And that you are His child…His masterpiece…Created in his image…

That will never change.

So…Rest assured.

If you believe…He is always there.

And your reward is not here…but in heaven.

And you can trust that your place there is reserved…

Reserved just for you.

Your name is on it.

So…rest easy…

None of it changes anything.

The Lesson of the Day.

It May Not Even Be Real

Good Morning, Brothers and Sisters.

"We look not to the things that are seen but to the things that are unseen. For the things that are seen are transient, but the things that are unseen are eternal" 2 Corinthians 4:18

"Now faith is the assurance of things hoped for, the conviction of things not seen." Hebrews 11: 1-3

"Everyone who lives in me, and believes in me, will never die." John 11:26

"Do not store up treasures for yourselves on earth…But store up treasures for yourselves in heaven." Matthew 6:19-20

It may not even be real.

I was texting with a woman last evening about an investment opportunity. She was an Italian woman (She sent me a picture, she appeared to be attractive, and she said she was from Rome, living in LA) who was trying to convince me to put some money into cryptocurrency. Something about the conversation bothered me. Clearly she was a believer in crypto. She was all in and pushing hard. We went back and forth with texting and because we were getting into the nitty-gritty I suggested that we move over to the phone, or meet in person and talk business. Nope. When I asked more questions about the crypto vehicle (as I was totally clueless) I learned that cryptocurrency is a virtual entity. It is actually not backed by anything, and only exists in the virtual, digital world. You can buy stuff with it…but only because our culture says this virtual thing has value. She argued that gold was the same…that gold only has value because our culture says it is valuable. It was a strange conversation…and after a while I asked myself if any of this was real. I wasn't sure. And, although I had this picture of an attractive woman with whom I was having this discussion…the picture mainly existed in my head. There was no way to know. She might be just creating this thing and I might be getting my chain yanked. So…after a while…I got my witts about me and thought better to make a respectful exist…and not do anything stupid.

So is any of this real?

In my line of work, facts support that a person weighs exactly the same the moment after they die as the moment before.

Is any of it real?

French philosopher Pierre Teilhard de Chardin wrote: "We are spiritual beings having a human experience."

And so it is…

We are ageless, spiritual beings created in the image of the Creator…the image of love.

And we were young once, and the house ages.

We only live there…

We are just fine…we don't need anything, but the house needs some paint and a roof.

So be careful… Don't be fooled...

Be careful where you invest…It may not even be real.

Our treasures are not here…but in heaven.

The Lesson of the Day.

It's All About Love

Good Morning, Brothers and Sisters.

It is all about love.

The whole journey.

All of it.

When Christ was asked which was the most important law, he responded with:

"Love God with your whole heart and love your neighbor as yourself." Matthew 22:37-39.

It's hard for some people to talk about love.

It's hard for some people to give and receive love.

Hollywood and our culture, and sometimes our families and our past, have messed it up.

You see…God is love. He is the source.

When you feel loved…you are feeling the presence of God.

God's Love is safe and secure…it is comforting, nurturing, and peaceful.

Here is what Paul says about love:

Love is patient and kind; it is not envious or conceited. It is not selfish or easily provoked.

Love finds joy in righteousness and in the truth.

It bears all things, believes and hopes in all things, and endures all things. Love never ends. 1 Corinthians 13

Love One Another.

Do it today.

The Lesson of the Day.

Jessica

Good Morning, Brothers and Sisters.

I don't define success as money or a prestigious job. It is not the car you drive or the house you own. It is fulfillment of your spirit...finding your purpose...discovering the reason you were sent here. It is believing so much in something that when you think of it your heart skips a beat with joy. A purpose that keeps you up at night...makes you push a little harder...makes you continue to knock on the door until it opens. Your purpose here...your" Mission from God" so to speak. Bigger and more important than any one thing. Able to stand on its own...and tall in the face of adversity. No one can take you down when you find it.

Jessica achieved something great yesterday. She was admitted to Nursing School at De Paul University in Chicago.

She had prepared herself over years for this moment. She should lavish in the achievement for a little while...and then get on with business. Seize the opportunity with endless passion and vigor. Don't be a regular nurse...but an extraordinary one. Expect a lot from yourself, and from those around you. Be of good service and don't settle...Don't settle for anything less than extraordinary.

Excellence means you need to be better than just good. Excellence with Humility, Kindness, and Love. A bright light in a dark place. They will know who you are not by what you say...but by what you do…the fruit that you bear. Lead by example and with empathy. In my view...this is success.

Nice work, Jessica!

Daddy could not be more proud of you, your hard work, and the woman you have become.

Now...go get it.

Lessons for Everybody... From Jessica

Tolerance

Good Morning, Brothers and Sisters.

"And as they continued to ask Him, He stood up and said to them: Let him who is without sin among you be the first to throw a stone at her." John 8:7

"Judge not, that you not be judged." Matthew 7:1

"Finally, all of you, have unity of mind, sympathy, brotherly love, a tender heart, and a humble mind. Do not repay evil for evil, but on the contrary, bless…for this is what you are called to do."
1 Peter 3: 8, 9

"…Let not one judge the other…for God has welcomed both."
Romans 14: 3

Might it be time to change the narrative?

Can you imagine accepting another's perspective as being as important as your own?

Imagine embracing and honoring our differences.

Imagine tolerance, acceptance, patience, goodness, and peace.

Imagine a respectful discussion of our differences.

Imagine being less critical.

Can we be more like Jesus?

"…Thy kingdom come, thy will be done, on Earth, as it is in Heaven."

Let's bring Heaven to Earth.

Let's bring love, tolerance, goodness, humility, sympathy, compassion, and peace to Earth.

Let's change the narrative.

Tolerance.

The Lesson of the Day.

Keep Your Eyes on Jesus.

Good Morning, Brothers and Sisters.

"Immediately after this, Jesus insisted that his disciples get back into the boat and cross to the other side of the lake while he sent the people home. After sending them home, he went up into the hills by himself to pray. Night fell while he was there alone. Meanwhile, the disciples were in trouble far away from the land, for a strong wind had risen and they were fighting heavy waves. About 3 o'clock in the morning, Jesus came toward them walking on the water. When the disciples saw him walking on the water, they were terrified. In their fear, they cried out: It's a ghost! But Jesus spoke to them at once: Do not be afraid. He said. Take courage…I am here. Then Peter called to him: Lord, if it's really you, tell me to come to you walking on the water. Yes…come. Jesus said. So Peter went over the side of the boat and walked on the water towards Jesus. But when he saw the strong wind and the waves he was terrified and began to sink. Save me Lord, He shouted. Jesus immediately reached out and grabbed him. You have so little faith, Jesus said: Why did you doubt me?"
Matthew 14:22-31

Stay focused on Christ.

Peter stepped out of the boat, focused on Christ, and was walking on the water… As all things are possible for those who believe.

The scripture does not suggest if Peter was amazed at what was happening.

I imagine that he was.

But we see next that Peter became distracted…he became scared by things happening around him…and he lost his focus on Christ.

And such is our walk through this earthly journey.

Storms abound…and trials are around every corner.

If we stay focused on Him, and with enough faith, we too are capable of incredible things.

Stay focused on Christ.

The Lesson of the Day.

Leo The Great

Good Morning, Brothers and Sisters.

"Those who spare the rod of discipline hate their children. Those who love their children care enough to discipline them."
Proverbs 13:24

"Honor your father and mother…Then you will live a long, full life in the land of the Lord." Exodus 20:12

"And you know that we treated each of you as a father treats his own children. We pleaded with you, encouraged you, comforted you, and urged you to live your lives in a way that God would consider worthy." 1 Thessalonians 2:11-12

"As for me and my family…we shall serve the Lord."
Joshua 24:15

Leo the Great.

He still brings a laughing smile to my face.

How lucky was I?

I could have had anybody as my dad…and I got him.

And how lucky was I?

But there were times…

Leo was a South-Philly Italian guy…

Who was a Marine.

Do you already have the picture?

He was tough, opinionated, and obnoxious.

He was funny…and always in my business…and my face.

And one more thing…he was always there…

Every game, every practice…all the time.

He demanded discipline…

And he expected excellence.

And if you delivered any less…he would let you know…

He didn't get crazy about it…but he would let you know.

I brought home a report card with 5 As and one B.

And he said…" What's the B?"

I did eventually get 6 As and he said "I knew you could do it."

Baseball was the same.

Life, and the rest of it, were the same…

That's what he expected.

And, you know, we were always in church…

And he was always volunteering at the little Catholic school where we went.

So…guess what happened…

I turned out pretty disciplined.

And I hope to always be there for my kids.

I achieved a fair amount in sports…

And in academics…

Although, I did have to learn that 93% was still an A. I hope to be a good man…

And a man of God…

And to be of service.

Turned out pretty good.

And I am thankful for him.

My dad Leo…

Leo the Great.

The Lesson of the Day.

Let Him Transform You

Good Morning, Brothers and Sisters.

"Do not conform to the pattern of this world, but be transformed into a new person by changing the way you think." Romans 12:2

"And we all, who with unveiled faces contemplate the Lord's glory, are being transformed into His glorious image, which comes from the Lord, who is the Spirit." 2 Corinthians 3:18

"The fruit of the Spirit is love, joy, peace, forgiveness, goodness, faithfulness, gentleness and self-control." Galatians 5:22, 23

Let Him transform you.

If you let Him, He will transform your mind, your heart, and your soul.

He will transform all of you…and you will become more Godly, more like Christ.

Your thoughts will be more wholesome and good.

Your outlook will be more positive…as He only has good things in mind for you.

Your heart and mind will be more at peace as His kingdom, and your home, are not of this world.

You will be kinder, more gentle and patient.

You will have a different perspective of everything.

You will bear good fruit.

And the darkness goes away with the light.

Let Him transform you.

The Lesson of the Day.

Let Your Light and Your Love Shine

Good Morning, Brothers and Sisters.

Ask any Emergency Room physician when all the action starts.

Ask any policeman when the most dangerous part of his shift is.

Evil hides in the shadows. You are prudent to be careful walking around that dark corner.

In Physics the definition of darkness is the absence of light. If we bring light into the darkness, the darkness goes away.

Light and darkness cannot exist at the same time.

"Then Jesus spoke to them again: 'I am the light of the world. Anyone who follows Me will never walk in darkness again…but have the light of life." John 8:12

"This is the message we have heard from Him: God is light and in Him there is no darkness. If we claim to have fellowship with Him yet walk in the darkness we are not living out of love and truth."
1 John 5-6

"You are the light of the world…like a city on a hilltop that cannot be hidden. No one lights a lamp and then puts it under a basket. Instead…a lamp is placed on a stand where it gives light to all in the house." Matthew 5 14-16

Our world needs bright lights…His light and your light. Jesus, through you, is the light of the world.

Let your light, your love, and your goodness shine brightly. Do it today.

The Lesson of the Day.

Life's Curves

Good Morning, Brothers and Sisters.

"Rejoice with those who rejoice; mourn with those who mourn." Romans: 12:15

"So with you: Now is your time of grief, but I will see you again and you will rejoice and no one will take away your joy." John 16:22

"Blessed are they that mourn…for they shall be comforted." Matthew 5:4

"I am the resurrection and the life…Anyone who lives in me and believes in me will never die." John 11:25-26

Sometimes life throws us a curve.

When I was a baseball player I could pick up the spin and give that curve a ride.

Life's curves are much more sneaky.

Problems at work…or home.

A marriage, or other important relationship, that gets off track..

Your children may be going sideways…

Or the doctor might have some distressing news.

Someone dies suddenly…or suffers longer with something dreadful.

A friend of mine, an Iron Man, went out with friends for his training ride and was hit by a car…

Instead of getting pizza and watching a movie…the family was busy with other things that evening.

Curves…

It might be a little breaker…

Or a big one…The big ones can buckle your knees.

So…be ready…be ready all the time.

Prepare.

Pray…with gratitude.

Be thankful for today and the moment at hand.

Talk to those important to you and make sure they know you love them.

Don't wait.

This life is temporary.

He assures us that if we believe in Him, we shall never die.

Keep your eyes on Him…and be ready…

Sometimes life throws us a curve.

The Lesson of the day.

Lisa

Good Morning, Brothers and Sisters.

I've had a little writer's block today, but some inspiration just came upon me. I was texting with a lifelong friend who lives in Texas. She recently had a bad fall and a terribly big injury. She fractured her femur and her arm. She had plates and screws placed for both and has been in a wheelchair since. She's now starting physical therapy.

The pain and disability have been grave.

There are no words to say when something like this happens.

She is lucky to have strong faith in God and a large family that surrounds her with love.

Love pushes the wheelchair.

Love brings the food and the water.

Love brings the ice when the pain is too great.

Love brings the medicine and fluffs the pillows.

Love holds her hand when it's too hard.

Love kisses her forehead and assures her that it is there with her.

Love heals.

The Lesson of the Day.

Loneliness

Good Morning, Brothers and Sisters.

"And be sure of this: I am with you always, even to the end of the age." Matthew 28:20

"For I am convinced that neither death nor life, neither angels nor demons, neither the present nor the future, nor any powers, neither height nor depth, nor anything else in all creation, will be able to separate us from the love of God that is in Christ Jesus our Lord" Romans 8:38-39

"Timothy, please come as soon as you can. Demas has deserted me because he loves the things of this life and gone to Thessalonica. Crescent has gone to Galatia, and Titus has gone to Dalmatia. Only Luke is with me. Bring Mark with you when you come…"
2 Timothy 4:9-11

Loneliness.

There will be seasons of loneliness.

He was near the end of his life…

And Paul felt abandoned and lonely.

We all go through it…

As part of our humanness.

A need to connect to others…

A need to be part of a larger body.

And a season where those needs go unmet.

A sense that no one is there…

Feeling isolated…

And alone.

It can mean no text or no call… Or an empty mailbox.

No one to listen… Or to care.

No one to receive your love…

And no one to give you love.

There will be seasons of loneliness…

And "It is not good for man to be alone."

Remember that God is always with you…always.

Change the perspective to one of peaceful, quiet solitude…and grow in Him.

That can be hard.

Be of service…

Volunteer…the Senior Center…the local hospital…or your church.

Thinking about others gets our minds off of ourselves.

Connect within your church…a small group or Bible study.

Exercise…exercise with other people exercising.

A social group…book club…a hiking group.

Stay in this moment…mindfulness…

Today, I noticed how my feet felt with every step.

Notice the birds…the littlest, smallest birds…and the trees…notice each leaf ruscelling in the breeze.

Call someone who might also be lonely…

And have gratitude for all of that.

The goal is no more loneliness.

The Lesson of the Day.

Look On the Other Side.

Good Morning, Brothers and Sisters.

"Throw your net on the right side of the boat and you will find some." John 21:6

"Do not conform to the pattern of this world, but be transformed by the renewing of your mind." Romans 12:2

"So we fix our eyes not on what is seen, but on what is unseen. For what is seen is temporary, but what is unseen is eternal."
2 Corinthians 4:18

"For my thoughts are not your thoughts, neither are your ways my ways, declares the Lord. And my ways are far beyond anything you might imagine." Isaiah 55:8

Look on the other side.

It may not appear to be the case…

But God's plan is unfolding all about us even now.

It may not be quite what we had in mind…but if we look closer, it is all there… All for our good…for our well-being.

And how is that?

Perhaps we just need to change the perspective…and look over there.

I was talking to a friend about prayer. She never said much about God and we rarely had this kind of conversation.

But…the question was "How does prayer work?"

We are told that God knew us before we were born and that our stories were written in His book long before we were around.

Do we believe that prayer can change God's plan for us?

Do we believe that we can change the will of God with our prayer?

That was the question.

The Bible says: Ask and you shall receive…seek and you will find…knock and the door will be opened.

At this moment I am growing…being tested…and another friend said to me: "Maybe you have to change where you are looking."

Although the friend that faced the question always avoided these discussions, she answered the question about prayer with: "I don't think that we change God's will, or His plan, with prayer. I think that prayer changes us…it changes our perspective…we look in another place where we find answers."

I think that she was more Godly than she even knew.

Change your perspective.

Our thoughts are not God's thoughts…or our ways His ways.

Be transformed…

Throw your net on the other side…

Look around…the answer may be right next to you.

Pray…

And change perspectives.

Find answers…

As they are unfolding all about us.

Look closer…

Next to you…maybe over there…

Look on the other side.

The Lesson of the Day.

Love and Light

Good Morning, Brothers and Sisters.

"Love the Lord your God with all your heart and all your soul and all your mind. This is the greatest and most important command. The second is like it. Love your neighbor as yourself." Mark 12:30-31

I ran into an older lady in a small restaurant in Kraków, Poland while there. She was an artist and gave me this picture.

Just as it was a few thousand years ago, it is today.

The people embraced Him for His message of goodness and love…but others hated Him for that same message.

The ruling class hated Him because He questioned them.

He brought light into their darkness, and they killed Him for it.

The messaging is still the same…

Light and darkness.

Choose light.

Let's take that message of light and love out there.

Let's do it today.

The Lesson of the Day.

Luke 6

Good Morning, Brothers and Sisters.

I read Luke Chapter 6 this morning and it is rich with life lessons.

Jesus heals on the Sabbath and asks the Pharisees if the law permits good deeds or bad deeds…saving life or destroying it…on the Sabbath.

He chooses 12 apostles:

Simon Peter, Andrew (Peter's brother), James (He may have been Jesus' step- brother), John, Philip, Bartholomew, Matthew (The Tax Collector), Thomas, another James, Simon the Zealot, Judas, and Judas Iscariat (who betrayed Him)

He teaches: Blessed are the Poor…for the Kingdom of God is theirs. Blessed are those who hunger…for they shall be satisfied. Blessed are those who weep…for they shall laugh. Blessings await you when people hate you because you follow the Son of Man. A great reward awaits you in heaven. Love your enemies…do good to those who hate you. What good is it if you only love those who love you? Be compassionate just as your Father is compassionate. Do not judge and you will not be judged…Why worry about the speck in your friend's eye when you have a log in your own? A good tree can not produce bad fruit and a bad tree can not produce good fruit. A tree is identified by its fruit.

A house built on a good foundation will withstand the floodwaters. A house built on a poor foundation will collapse in ruins.

Many Rich Lessons for Today…From the Son of Man.

Miracles

Good Morning, Brothers and Sisters.

"There are only two ways to live your life. One is as though nothing is a miracle. The other is as though everything is a miracle."

Albert Einstein-

The Lesson of the Day

MLK I

Good Morning, Brothers and Sisters.

"We are to resist using violence even in retaliation for violence used against us." Luke 6:29

"Do not repay evil with evil." 1 Peter 3:9

"But there is something I must say to my people who stand on the warm threshold that leads into the palace of justice. In the process of gaining our rightful place, we must not be guilty of wrongful deeds. Let us not seek to satisfy our thirst for freedom by drinking from the cup of bitterness and hatred." Martin Luther King.

Important instructions after the events of the weekend.

Remember…It's only us.

The Lesson of the Day.

MLK II

Good Morning, Brothers and Sisters.

"Make every effort to live in peace with everyone and to be holy; without holiness, no one will see the Lord." Hebrews 12:14

"So God created mankind in his own image, and in the image of God He created them." Genesis 1:27

"Love one another. As I loved you, so you must love one another." John 13:34

"Five score years ago, a great American, in whose symbolic shadow we stand today, signed the Emancipation Proclamation. This momentous decree came as a great beacon light of hope to millions of Negro slaves who had been seared in flames of withering injustice. It came as a joyous daybreak to end the long night of their captivity. We must forever conduct our struggle on the high plain of dignity and discipline. We must not allow our creative protest to degenerate into physical violence. The marvelous new militancy which has engulfed the Negro community must not lead us to distrust all white people, for many of our white brothers, as evidenced by their presence here today, have come to realize that their destiny is tied to our destiny, and their freedom is bound to our freedom." Martin Luther King

"There is no us and them…only us."

Father Joe Carroll, Father Joe's Villages, at lunch.

Remember…It's only us.

The Lesson of the Day.

Multiply the Fish

Good Morning, Brothers and Sisters.

"This is a remote place, and it's already getting late. Send the crowds away so they can go to the villages and buy food for themselves. But Jesus said, "That isn't necessary…you feed them."

"But we have only five loaves of bread and two fish."

"Bring them here," He said. Then He told the people to sit down. Jesus took the five loaves and two fish, looked up to heaven, and blessed them. Then, breaking the loaves into pieces, He gave the bread to the disciples, who distributed it to the people." Matthew 14:15-19

"About this time another large crowd had gathered and the people had run out of food again. Jesus called to his disciples and said: "I feel sorry for these people. They have been here with me for three days, and they have nothing to eat. If I send them home hungry, they will faint along the way, for some of them have come a long distance." His disciples replied, "How are we supposed to find enough food to feed them out here in the wilderness?"

Jesus asked: "How much bread do you have?" "Seven loaves," they replied.

So Jesus told the crowd to sit down and he took the seven loads and thanked God for them. He broke the bread into pieces and had his disciples distribute them to the crowd. A few small fish were found, and he blessed them and had the disciples distribute them."
Mark 8:1-7

Multiply the Fish

We are entering a time of year that some welcome…and others dread.

It is the political season and we are challenged to sort out the flooding information coming at us from both sides.

For many of us…it gets old really quick… And what's the point any way?

We each have one vote and what difference will that make?

The pastor at our church gave a sermon about this last Sunday and I feel it bears repeating.

To many our country has become something we barely recognize.

It seems that none of it has been the will of the people…but the will of a select few.

God has anointed our country throughout history.

This country…logically… shouldn't even be here.

The United States has been threatened, and maybe should have gone away, many times.

And only by the grace of God…

And how is it that the bullet only got his ear?

Only by the grace of God…and the angel.

He multiplied the fish and the loaves… And votes?

Can He make one vote into lots of votes?

He certainly can do it…

And both parties wish they could master that trick.

He is watching over this country.

We can depend on Him…

He can really do it…

Be sure to vote…make sure you do… It will count…

Remember…

He multiplied the Fish.

The Lesson of the Day.

Nick the Sniper

Good Morning, Brothers and Sisters.

"I have told you all of this so that you may have peace in me. Here on earth you will have many trials and sorrows. But take heart, because I have overcome the world." John 16:33

"Soldiers, don't get tied up in the affairs of the civilian life…for then they cannot please the officer who enlisted them." 2 Timothy 2:4

"This is my command…be strong and courageous! Do not be afraid or be discouraged. For the Lord your God is with you wherever you go." Joshua 1:9

"Therefore, put on every piece of God's armor so that you will be able to resist the enemy in the time of evil." Ephesians 6:13

"The Lord gives his people strength. The Lord blesses them with peace." Psalm 29:11

Nick the Sniper

I was in the Ukraine with a small medical team a few months after war broke out with Russia. We were part of a larger relief effort near LVIV's train station providing refugees with necessary goods and services as they tried to escape war and make their way to Poland. The medical issues were pretty simple but the emotional toll that war was taking on the people was extreme.

We spent about a week in LVIV and then went back to Krakow, Poland preparing to return to the US. I was rooming with an ER nurse from San Diego and I was set to meet him to get some dinner after our arrival. When I went to the restaurant area, I saw my friend sitting at the bar with someone. As I approached and overheard the conversation, the guy was clearly an American, and clearly was very upset.

His name was Nick.

We later called him Nick the Sniper.

Nick was from Michigan and was a retired Marine sniper. He had been contacted by a military contractor asking if he was interested in fighting on Ukraine's behalf. After some brief negotiations regarding equipment and team members, Nick agreed to again be a warrior.

We met Nick that night.

Nick was very upset and tearful.

He told us the story:

Nick was commanding a small group of 10 men fighting in eastern Ukraine. He saw 4 of his men killed and should have been killed himself. Nick took a round in the middle of his chest and was saved by his body armor. He told us that he saw things that he had never seen in his long military career. He had served in Afghanistan and Iraq and was involved in many battles. Nothing compared to what he had seen In Ukraine. He saw civilians…families…lined up and killed. He saw Russian tanks firing at an apartment building full of people. He saw lots of innocent lives taken. He saw the nonsense, the senselessness of war.

We spent about 4 hours talking with Nick. We did our best to comfort him…but there were no words.

What was there to say?

Nick was a brave, brave man…a warrior…who saw the worst of our humanity. Is there anything worse than war?

And how is it that a few people's egos, and power, and greed…can let us do this to each other?

And how is it that we have learned nothing after all the years…from the beginning of time…except how to kill each other more efficiently?

This war won't be the last war.

And Nick won't be the last to suffer from war…and tell the stories of war.

We can only change that which we can.

We can put lots of love on each other.

Pray for our leaders…for common sense…and to stop the killing.

Pray for the people affected by war.

Help them when you can.

Touch each life with love and goodness.

You see…love and goodness are contagious.

Let's pray harder to bring the peace of heaven to earth…

And to understand that it is not about who wins or loses…

As we all lose with war.

You see…it is only us.

The Lesson of the Day.

One Body, One story

Good Morning, Brothers and Sisters.

"There is no longer Jew or Greek, there is no longer slave or free, there is no longer male and female; for all of you are one in Christ Jesus." Galatians 3:28

"And Jesus replied: I tell you the truth…when you do it to the least of your brothers and sisters…you have done it to me." Matthew 25:40

"Yes there are many parts, but only one body. The eye can never say to the hand…I don't need you; and the head can't say to the feet…I don't need you…All of you together are Christ's body and each of you is a part of it." 1 Corinthians 20, 21, 27

There is one body… And there is one story.

In the late 1700s astronomers and mathematicians were able to discover equations that were predictive of the orbits of the known planets. Direct observations of those orbits seemed to be in conflict with those mathematical predictions. This conflict remained unexplained leading many to hypothesize that there was another, yet undiscovered planet, whose gravity was affecting those orbits.

In 1846 Neptune was discovered in a part of the sky where those calculations predicted it would be.

It is all the same story…

And just as the hand and the foot are of the same body…

We are of the body of Christ.

And each part affects the other…

The body feels pain as the foot steps in the wrong place.

The whole body suffers when there is heartache.

And what is the effect of any individual's bad decisions on the moral compass of our society?

The whole world suffers when there is hunger, conflict, or war.

And the tides are affected by the phases of the moon…

And our atmosphere by things on the sun..

The Old Testament is the history of Israel…and its stories are all predictive of a servant-king named Jesus.

It is all one story…

The story started "In the Beginning…"

His story…

Our story….

The same story.

And everything affects everything else…

It is only Him.

It is only us…

One body…One story.

The Lesson of the Day.

Only by the Grace of God

Good Morning, Brothers and Sisters.

I'm sitting here out back with my coffee as I usually do in the morning.

The dogs are running around and having fun and it's another beautiful Southern California day. There are no clouds in the sky and there's a very light breeze…a beautiful start. This message is going to be a little different. It's going to be just one of those stream of thought things. I'm so thankful that I get to sit here and wonder and think, pray and ponder…God…life…and it's ups and downs.

I've been so blessed through the journey…I look back in amazement at all of it. The story starts with baseball…I still dream of it several times a week. I love that game and it is part of my fabric.

God gave me gifts there.

I could throw it and I could catch it.

I was decent at the plate and, although no one would ever call me fast, I ran pretty well.

I was a catcher. I was strong and smart…and I had a good grasp of the game.

The game introduced me to lots of people who remain my friends today.

It enabled me to go to college and get an education.

We even played for a national championship.

Although some of my friends went on to play professionally, my baseball career ended that night…

It was a Monday night.

There was no more practice and no more games.

It was a dark time when baseball ended.

An important relationship ended at about the same time.

It was dark.

I struggled. I was depressed. It was hard.

But I was lucky that God and I remained close.

That dark time lasted a while, but soon God started working on me with this medicine thing. He wouldn't leave me alone with it. It turned out to be the reason I was sent to the earth. It was at that time that I started to understand how God's plan, and His timing, works…and why baseball had to go away. I did well in medical school and loved the work. I finished my career after 30-something years…about half of that with the indigent and underserved, and the rest with regular folks. Along the way came three beautiful children and a marriage that eventually failed because of stupid stuff on both sides.

And now I'm in the next part of the journey.

I'm waiting on God once again to answer some questions.

God and I are closer now.

The next part of the journey has some unanswered questions.

There are relationship questions.

There are professional questions…how do I continue to be of service?

There's always the aging thing…

And other stuff…

Many things to think about… And to navigate.

I need to remember that He has a great plan…

He had it all mapped out before I was even around. He knows me and what I need…better than I do.

He gave me many gifts.

I have to wait on him and trust him…just like before.

His plans for me are magnificent, and greater than I might imagine.

Those answers are already mine.

I have to pray, and wait.

And more important…not do anything stupid in my impatience to get answers.

This probably sounds familiar to many of you.

Successes, failures, trials, waiting…

and waiting some more.

Much of what I am is the result of things I learned from the trials and failures.

They made me grow up.

I matured.

I became a man.

They taught me resilience and fortitude.

I had to decide what I really believed and what I stood for.

I had to find my life's purpose.

I had to decide about my relationship with God.

I had to decide how I was going to use my gifts.

So…the real Blessings were not all the successes…but the failures and the trials…

And the lessons they taught.

Those failures and trials brought me here. I was blessed with them.

It turned out better than good…

Only by the grace of God.

The Lesson of the Day.

www.ingramcontent.com/pod-product-compliance
Lightning Source LLC
Chambersburg PA
CBHW041330120726
48005CB00014B/2195